Growing the Vocabulary of English-Language Learners

Growing the Vocabulary of English-Language Learners

A Starter Kit for Classroom Teachers

Melissa Parenti, Danielle DiMarco,
and E. Francine Guastello

ROWMAN & LITTLEFIELD
Lanham • Boulder • New York • London

Published by Rowman & Littlefield
An imprint of The Rowman & Littlefield Publishing Group, Inc.
4501 Forbes Boulevard, Suite 200, Lanham, Maryland 20706
www.rowman.com

Unit A, Whitacre Mews, 26-34 Stannary Street, London SE11 4AB

British Library Cataloguing in Publication Information Available

Library of Congress Cataloging-in-Publication Data

Names: Parenti, Melissa, 1975- author. | DiMarco, Danielle, 1978- author. | Guastello, E. Francine, 1952- author.
Title: Growing the vocabulary of English language learners : a starter kit for classroom teachers / Melissa Parenti, Danielle DiMarco, and E. Francine Guastello.
Description: Lanham, Maryland : Rowman & Littlefield, [2018] | Includes bibliographical references.
Identifiers: LCCN 2018007362 (print) | LCCN 2018022476 (ebook) | ISBN 9781475818345 (electronic) | ISBN 9781475818338 (pbk. : alk. paper)
Subjects: LCSH: Vocabulary—Study and teaching. | English language—Study and teaching—Foreign speakers.
Classification: LCC PE1449 (ebook) | LCC PE1449 .P299 2018 (print) | DDC 428.1071—dc23
LC record available at https://lccn.loc.gov/2018007362

Printed in the United States of America

These ideas are dedicated to all of the PK–12 educators working countless engaging hours teaching, planning, and refining their practice with the aim of assuring that all students meet success.

Contents

Introduction

Although there are many critical elements to consider when working to improve the achievement of English-language learners (ELLs), there is one particular facet of instruction that is frequently noted as paramount by classroom teachers and researchers alike. More impressively, it has proven effective with great consistency over the course of time. It is vocabulary.

Vocabulary is the key to our understanding of conversations and text. Therefore, vocabulary is well-revered in the educational arena as the prerequisite for reading comprehension (August, McCardle, and Shanahan 2014). There is wide recognition of this link between comprehension and vocabulary knowledge; it has been noted that ELLs who experience struggles with vocabulary development and maintain a limited English vocabulary often have issues with comprehension (August, Carlo, Dressler, and Snow 2005, 50).

For this specific reason, vocabulary, with targeted intentional attention on Tier II and academic vocabulary, has become the dominant emphasis in working with ELLs in our everyday classrooms (Beck, McKeown, and Kucan 2002). Academic vocabulary, the type of language that is fundamental for school-based success, is generally not used outside of the classroom, involves complex sentence structures, and has multiple forms not typically practiced in nonacademic environments. Further, it is the most difficult to attain (Goldenberg 2008, 13).

In his renowned ELL work, Cummins (1994) emphasized this consequential role of academic vocabulary in the development of second-language learning. He characterized acquisition of basic interpersonal communicative skills (BICS) and cognitive academic language proficiency (CALP) (Cummins 1994). He argued, "Educators and policy-makers frequently conflated conversational and academic dimensions of English language proficiency and that this conflation contributed significantly to the creation of academic difficulties for students who were learning English as an additional language (EAL)" (Cummins, 2008, 3).

As many classroom teachers will share, there is great truth in this finding. English-Language Learners frequently show mastery of basic communication skills and are heard expressing themselves with great clarity in conversations on the playground and in the cafeteria, but they are left laboring when the demands of classroom instruction are presented in Tier II or academic language. Cummins (1984) drew attention to this discrepancy and the need for classroom teachers to address CALP or the academic language that allows for students to access content in a learning setting.

Additionally, Beck and McKeown (2008) worked to support classroom teachers and decisions about instruction related to this high priority and fundamental academic language or vocabulary. They designed a framework as a guide when searching for high yield, or the most-promising academic vocabulary words to teach. Within their framework, vocabulary words are categorized as Tier I, Tier II, and Tier III.

Tier I words are those commonly used words already familiar to the student. Tier II words are referred to as high-utility words or those most frequently found across multiple contexts and content areas. Tier III are content specific. For this reason, Tier II words become the focal point and produce the largest benefits because they include those words most frequently encountered in academic settings across all disciplines (Beck and McKeown 2008).

As classroom teachers, though, we often feel that we could spend our entire school days filled with instruction of Tier II and academic vocabulary words. This often reminds us of the pivotal beginning phases of a young child's life. Research has, unfortunately, revealed a great discrepancy when comparing vocabulary development among professional, working class, and welfare families (Hart and Risely 1993). Hart and Risely (1993) report, at age four, an average child in a professional family experiences almost 45 million words; an average child in a working class family 26 million words; and an average child in a welfare family 13 million words.

Keith Stanovich (1986) also reinforced the magnitude of this data when he introduced the Matthew effect in reading. Here, he noted, "Children with inadequate vocabularies—who read slowly and without enjoyment—read less, and as a result have slower development of vocabulary knowledge, which inhibits further growth in reading ability" (Stanovich 1986, 381). This research only further reinforces the tremendous impact we have on our students' academic success and just how influential vocabulary development is on all subsequent aspects of reading and learning.

As a result, it has become even more detrimental for enriched vocabulary instruction when working with English-Language Learners, many of which are from homes of various socioeconomic status and homes with a predominant language other than English.

So how do we best teach the demanding, yet critical, Tier II and academic vocabulary to ELLs? The answer resides in the research, where two practices appear repetitively in the data. These favorable practices are explicit instruction of each new word and the provision of ongoing multiple exposures to this new vocabulary.

It has been found that ELLs learning to read in English are similar to English speakers learning to read in English; they benefit from explicit teaching of vocabulary (Goldenberg 2008). And as many researchers cite, the vocabulary research significantly highlights the need for multiple exposures or frequent encounters with new words if they are to become a permanent part of an individual's long-standing vocabulary (Beck and McKeown, 2008).

This text is designed to introduce and model explicit instruction and multiple exposures to Tier II and academic vocabulary and lend a helping hand to classroom teachers working day in and day out to support English-Language Learners in a positive and academically and socially rewarding way. The work that follows briefly introduces the theory and a framework supporting explicit instruction of new vocabulary and includes teacher-friendly research substantiating the push for multiple exposures to these new words.

Additionally, a series of strategies to allow for multiple exposures to new vocabulary accompanied by a mini-lesson designed to launch each instructional tool, as well as strategies for promoting morphological awareness are provided. As we begin our journey to improve vocabulary instruction for ELLs, our aim is to improve not only the quantity of opportunities for thoughtful vocabulary work, but also, more importantly, the quality of the tasks (Gersten and Baker 2000; Manyak and Bouchereau 2009).

Chapter One

Explicit Instruction of Vocabulary

Not only is selection of appropriate vocabulary essential, but also is the need for quality instruction as new words are introduced (Gersten and Baker 2000). Research highlights various qualities present when effective vocabulary instruction is taking place, and yet, pivotal in research is the need for direct, explicit instruction and multiple exposures as English-language learners (ELLs) are introduced to new vocabulary.

Incidental learning of vocabulary has proven less effective for ELLs, which calls on educators to assure the provision of straightforward, explicit instruction of intentionally introduced words (August, McCardle, and Shanahan 2014; Blachowicz, Fisher, Ogle, and Watts-Taffe 2006; Carlo, August, McLaughlin, Snow, Dressler, Lippman, Lively, and White 2004). Efficient student acquisition of new vocabulary, therefore, is reliant on instruction that is far removed from the archaic practice of locating and writing the definition of new words in a notebook.

It is the use of explicit instruction with vocabulary that can increase learning and ultimately greater comprehension of text (McKeown and Beck 2003). Direct instruction continues to produce indication of word learning and requires active participation from both teacher and student (Loftus and Coyne 2012).

Why is explicit instruction so essential? Lehr, Osborn, and Hiebert (2011) note that explicit instruction is a must for ELLs because it has the capacity—through clear explanations and formative assessment with the provision of feedback—to assure that the vocabulary being taught is understood. Explicit instruction is productive because it is focused and not only provides the explanation of new words, but also guided analysis of word meanings that allow for in-depth comprehension of new vocabulary and applicability to varying texts and content (Shanahan 2006).

Direct or explicit instruction is rooted in the work of Rosenshine (1983) with slight revisions by reading researchers Pearson and Gallagher (1983). Pearson and Gallagher (1983) introduced the gradual-release model as a route for assuring that instruction was explicit. A gradual-release model is centered on the idea that the instructor gradually releases control of the lesson as student mastery becomes more evident. As students work toward mastery, they gradually acquire more control over their learning and understanding of the new content.

Instruction that is gradual and explicit, therefore, requires that the instructor, first, demonstrate the new content (Pearson and Gallagher 1983). Next, a guided practice phase ensues, during which time the instructor allows for all learners to engage with the new content in a manner that serves as progress monitoring and provides evidence of student learning.

It is during this critical guided segment of the lesson that the instructor is able to check for student understanding and provide feedback specific to the learning needs (Pearson and Gallagher 1983). If sufficient progress is made, the instructor moves the learner to the independent practice portion of the lesson that is completed autonomously and with minimal teacher support.

Explicit instruction via a gradual-release model continues to be touted as the most effective route when teaching new vocabulary to ELLs (Carlo et al. 2004; August, McCardle, and Shanahan 2014). When vocabulary instruction is explicit, the teacher is clear about the definition of new words. There is no confusion related to the word's actual meaning or endless dictionary searches that steal valuable instructional minutes. It is efficient and accurate.

Additionally, after the meaning of each new word is clear, student-friendly definitions and explanations are provided by the teacher (Beck, McKeown, and Kucan 2013). It is these relatable explanations that connect the world of ELLs to the vocabulary they encounter. These descriptions introduce typical uses of the word and explain the meaning in everyday language (Cronbach 1942).

Although the initial phase of explicit vocabulary instruction appears teacher centric, students gradually gain ownership over their learning. It is once understanding of the new words exists that students are held accountable for reading, writing, listening, and speaking the words (Shanahan 2006). For this reason, lessons in explicit instruction provide ample opportunity for students to apply the new knowledge in ways that reveal student mastery of the new vocabulary.

It is this evidence of student understanding that ultimately drives the instruction forward to independent practice when mastery has been attained or backward for reteaching when mastery is limited.

Explicit instruction of vocabulary not only takes place when new words are introduced but also when equipping students for vocabulary success outside of the classroom setting. This out-of-class success is reliant on the notion that students are able to recognize and apply the most-efficient routes for exploring new vocabulary. These routes are known as *word-learning strategies* and are used by learners as a vehicle for acquiring meanings of new words based on context and morphological patterns.

As a result, explicit instruction is also used as a route for assisting students in obtaining and mastering these word-learning strategies (Vaughn, Dimmino, Schumm, and Bryant 2001). These strategies engage students in their reflection of new words, word structure and meaning, and association to other words they may know. More specifically, use of these word-learning strategies provide learners with a framework or structure for acquiring word meanings through context and morphology (Carlo et al. 2004).

The strategies presented within this text serve as models or the initial phase of a gradual-release model and a demonstration of supporting ELLs through explicit instruction in word learning. These strategies provide a scaffold or support for ELLs when new words are encountered inside and outside of a classroom setting and are designed to assist in the ongoing accessibility and knowledge of new vocabulary encountered when acquiring a second language.

It is this repository of strategies designed to increase vocabulary and self-regulated learning that holds great promise for improving achievement for ELLs in all content areas (Zimmerman and Schunk 2001).

Chapter Two

Multiple Exposures to Vocabulary

In addition to the abundance of research noting the values of explicit instruction of new vocabulary, is a similar dominance in data supporting the need for English-language learners (ELLs) to experience multiple exposures to new vocabulary (Blachowicz et al. 2006). Frequent encounters with new words assists in establishing a firm grasp on the meaning of new words and eventually embeds the words in an individual's vocabulary repertoire (McKeown and Kucan 2002). These frequent encounters, or multiple exposures, provide opportunities for application of the new vocabulary in many ways and are not designed as simply repetitive drill of the words, but rather, thoughtful interactions with words across multiple contexts (Stahl 2005; Stanley and Ginther 1991).

With increased attention on promoting achievement for English-Language Learners, the concept of multiple exposures to new vocabulary is continuously underscored. Providing a higher number of encounters with vocabulary has shown to be effective in producing word-learning outcomes (McKeown, Beck, Omanson, and Pople 1985). Additionally, multiple exposures have the potential to make an even greater impact on student achievement when they are meaningful, relatable, and allow for authentic associations to be linked to the new vocabulary (Beck et al. 1985).

Associations occur during assorted interactions with the word, which also provide exposure to variance in meaning based on concept and the content (Nagy and Scott 2000). Instructionally, these multiple associations occur after explicit instruction of new vocabulary takes place. They are revisits of the words initially taught. Multiple exposures and interactions with words can be formal or informal in nature. Often, though, they take shape as a form of word play or playful interaction with words.

5

Students who engage with words by hearing them, using them, manipulating them semantically, and playing with them are more likely to retain new vocabulary (Blachowicz and Fisher 2008). Multiple exposures in meaningful and playful ways counteract the monotony of age-old word searches and matching practice simply associating words and their definitions and improves overall word learning (Nagy and Scott 2000; Graves 2008).

Research continues to urge that instruction move beyond minimal surface-level teaching and learning, especially as it relates to vocabulary instruction for ELLs (Cummins 2008; Gersten and Baker 2000). As you will discover within the strategies in this text, providing multiple exposures through word-play activities accomplishes the task and provides an increased quantity and engaging quality of instruction for ELLs while also furthering vocabulary growth.

Chapter Three

Implementation and the Strategies

IMPLEMENTATION

This book has been designed with the intent of providing English-language learners (ELLs) with explicit instruction of vocabulary and word-learning strategies, as well as multiple exposures to new words. Not only does the gradual-release model of explicit instruction apply to vocabulary lessons for ELLs, but it also applies when training preservice and in-service educators. For this reason, each word-learning strategy has been designed in a manner that serves as a demonstration or model of each best practice and plays the role of supporting teachers as each strategy is introduced.

Each lesson begins with an "Introduce and Connect" segment that allows for the teachers to link day-to-day learning, as well as access to student prior knowledge. Once this thoughtful revisit and introduction takes place, the lesson moves into a momentum based gradual-release sequence designed to lessen teacher responsibility and increase student responsibility. As the lesson moves forward, momentum is driven by student engagement and evidence of understanding.

This effective sequence begins with the "I Do" segment. Here, the teacher explains the strategy with clarity and demonstrates a model of the strategy in use. Research of ELLs has proven that more new vocabulary is acquired when this phase of direct teaching occurs (Goldenberg 2008). This critical step not only introduces the new content, but also vocalizes the instructional intent and values for the student and serves as a replica of the expected product.

Once the intent or objective of the lesson has been shared, the next phase involves teacher-supported guided practice. This is the "We Do" segment.

Here, student engagement is at the center of all activity. Thus, all students are actively engaged, not merely those volunteering their participation.

Lessons are also equipped with teacher prompts for accountable student talk with partners. It is during this guided practice portion of the lesson that the teacher is not only directing conversations, but also listening and monitoring students' understanding with the provision of feedback. For this reason, Checkpoint #1 is located within the "We Do." This is where the teacher assesses the level of accuracy in attaining the intended instructional outcome, often referred to as *formative assessment.*

The results of Checkpoint #1 then guide the lesson forward or backward based on student understanding. If sufficient progress has not been made, the lesson moves back into a phase of "I Do" in which the teacher reteaches the material and siphons out any misunderstandings. If sufficient progress has been made, the lesson moves into the independent practice, or "You Do," phase of the lesson.

During the "You Do" or independent practice, each student is asked to display individual evidence of learning. Within each lesson, the words *on your own* appear with frequency. Student learning for all learners is the desired outcome of each lesson. Therefore, this is the crucial moment within the lesson where the teacher steps back from leading and guiding and allows each student to practice independently. Allowing students to practice independently is the only way to truly assure that the "I Do" and "We Do" were successful for every learner.

At the close of the lesson, students are invited to share their learning or show what they know. It is within this step that Checkpoint #2 occurs. The results of Checkpoint #2 are telling and reveal evidence of mastery, partial mastery, or limited mastery of the strategy that was introduced. Checkpoint #2 serves as a summative measure of student progress.

Although direct instruction via a gradual release is highly promising, there are always differences in student learning and acquisition of new content. With this in mind, each lesson also contains specific, research-based scaffolds for ELLs. These scaffolds include opportunities to support language production (Krashen 1982).

Additionally, embedded within each lesson are specific sentence frames to encourage reinforcement of various forms (structure of the word and how it shifts) and functions (purpose for use of the word and how it shifts) of new words (Krashen 1987). Finally, at the close of each lesson are leveled questions crafted to provide opportunities for output of language related to new content or vocabulary attained within the lesson (Krashen 1987). Most importantly, these lessons were designed for learning, but also student and teacher enjoyment.

Mini-lesson Title: Context Connection

Questions to keep in mind:
* Assessment: How will I know if the students have achieved the goal of the lesson? What will I observe or collect?
* Lesson Checkpoint #1 (During the Lesson): Am I actively engaging all learners? What evidence will I look for (observation) to assess if the students are meeting the goal of the lesson?
* Lesson Checkpoint #2 (At the end of independent work time/Exit Slip): What evidence will I collect to assess if the students are meeting the goal of the lesson?

Lesson Segment	Teaching Moves (Instruction may sound like . . .)	Language Production Sentence Frames
Introduce and Connect	"When I was an elementary student, my teachers would choose all of my vocabulary words from the stories or content area textbooks my class would read together. When we didn't recognize or understand a word when we read, the teacher would tell my class to use clues from the sentence to take our best guess at what the word means." "Those clues are called *context clues*. From experience, I can tell you that using context clues would help me figure out the meaning of an unfamiliar word in a sentence, but it never helped me add the word to the storage in my mind so that I could use it in my conversations and writing." "Today I want to show you an even better way to learn new words found in context and help you remember what they mean. We will do this by predicting word meanings using context clues, confirming or revising the predicted word meaning during a class discussion of its actual meaning, and finally, making a connection to a clue that will help us understand and remember the meaning of the word." "It's easy to remember those three steps if we use the Context Connection graphic organizer to guide us!"	Context clues are . . .

(continued)

Lesson Segment	Teaching Moves (Instruction may sound like . . .)	Language Production Sentence Frames
I DO (Teacher models)	"Pay close attention because I'm going to show you how I use the graphic organizer before you try it on your own. Let's look at the first word in context. The sentence says 'The queen welcomed the guests to her ball in a dignified manner.' I notice that the word *dignified* is highlighted in bold font and is underlined. That is my target vocabulary word." "If I move to the second column it says 'I think the word means . . .' Hmm, using the clues from the sentence I can predict that the word *dignified* means polite. I think that because a queen usually acts in a polite way. Let me add that to my graphic organizer." "At this point in the lesson, after everyone makes their predictions and jots them down we will have a class discussion about the actual meaning of the word(s). For today's demonstration my teacher helper, Grace (student volunteer) is going to define the word using the dictionary and give me a few examples of ways it can be used." *(Grace provides a definition and a few examples.)* "Great! Now I know what the word really means. My teacher says it means showing or acting in a very formal, serious, or reserved way. My prediction was pretty close. Let me jot down the actual definition in my own words in column 3." "Last, I need to think of a connection or a clue to help me remember and understand what *dignified* means. The first person that pops in my head is Princess Kate. She is an example of a person who acts *dignified*. Let me write that down right away so I don't forget it."	When I use the Context Connection graphic organizer, I . . . First, I . . . Next, I . . . Finally, I . . .

WE DO (Teacher guides, supports, and assesses) *Lesson Checkpoint #1*	"How about all of you try one now? Let's look down to the next example of a word in context. The next sentence says, 'The team worked together to conquer the opponent.' Notice that the word *opponent* is highlighted in bold font and is underlined."	The target word is . . . . The sentence is . . . . My predicted meaning is . . . The real definition of the word is . . . . My prediction was . . . .
	"Talk with your partner for a minute to try and predict what the word *opponent* means in this sentence." (Teacher listens in on partner conversations and provides coaching to guide the students.)"	
	"Tyler and Deanna used the clues in the sentence to help them predict that the word *opponent* means the people a team challenges or plays a game against. That makes sense. Let me add that to my Context Connection graphic organizer in the second column."	
	"Now let's discuss the actual meaning of the word *opponent*. *Opponent* means someone you compete against. In the sentence the team worked together to conquer the opponent. Perhaps they worked together by using all of their skills to win the game."	
	"OK. Again, turn and discuss with your partner what the word *opponent* really means. Was your prediction close or way off? Also, think of a clue that can help you connect your understanding of what the word means to your long-term memory. (*Teacher listens to partnership interactions once again to identify which students may need additional support.*)	
	(*Teacher shares student responses and adds several to the Context Connection graphic organizer displayed for the class.*)	
	* *Lesson Checkpoint #1:* Ask yourself, "Am I actively engaging all learners? Are the students demonstrating the ability to complete the task and meet the goal of the lesson with peer and teacher support?"	

(continued)

Lesson Segment	Teaching Moves (Instruction may sound like . . .)	Language Production Sentence Frames
YOU DO (Teacher supports through individual and small group differentiated instruction and assesses students) *Lesson Checkpoint #2	"You all did such a fantastic job! Now you can go off to try a few more on your own. We will gather again in a little while to share our graphic organizers with our partners, small groups, etc." Student completes the activity individually. Students who display evidence of needing additional assistance can be provided with a brief targeted reteach of the activity or key concepts within the activity based on the data gathered during *Lesson Checkpoint 1.	
SHARE *Lesson Checkpoint #2	Teacher structures a brief opportunity for students to share their work with the group.	

At the heart of this work is student achievement and explicit instruction and attainment of word-learning strategies designed to assist ELLs' encounters with new vocabulary. It is our hope that you and your students enjoy the work as much as we do. We adore teaching and learning and have created this text to breathe a bit of energy, efficiency, and positive outcome into our everyday practice supporting ELLs.

LIMITED ENGLISH PROFICIENCY: LEVELED QUESTION SUPPORTS

Point to the target word. Point to a context clue.

Find the sentence with the word. Read the sentence.

Match the target word to one of these words. (Teacher provides list of synonyms as options.)

Place the target word next to one of these words that defines it. (Teacher provides list of synonyms as options.)

Is ___(target word)___ , ___(synonym)___ or ___(synonym)___ ?

(Biemiller and Boote 2006; Chung 2012)

Context Connection

Word in Context	I think the word means . . .	The dictionary defines the word as . . .	How could I define this word if I tried to explain it to a friend?

(Biemiller and Boote, 2006)

Mini-lesson Title: Guess My Word

Questions to keep in mind:
* Assessment: How will I know if the students have achieved the goal of the lesson? What will I observe or collect?
* Lesson Checkpoint #1 (During the Lesson): Am I actively engaging all learners? What evidence will I look for (observation) to assess if the students are meeting the goal of the lesson?
* Lesson Checkpoint #2 (At the end of independent work time/Exit Slip): What evidence will I collect to assess if the students are meeting the goal of the lesson?

Lesson Segment	Teaching Moves (Instruction may sound like . . .)	Language Production Sentence Frames
Introduce and Connect	"We have been working on using and revisiting many new vocabulary words this year. One way that we can learn more and figure out which words we know well and which words we need to work on is by playing the game 'Guess My Word'."	
I DO (Teacher models)	"Before you have a chance to play the game with your group, I want you to take a moment to watch me demonstrate how to play with my friends, Sophie, Alex, and Eduardo. I want you to notice that the clue cards have been filled out for every word we have learned this year. I also want you to watch closely to see that all of the cards are placed blank side up in the middle of each group."	An noun is . . . A verb is . . . An adjective is . . . A syllable is . . . When I play the Guess My Word game, I . . .
	"I want you to watch closely as I begin the game by picking up a card. I read reach clue slowly until a group member guesses the target word."	
	"Whoever guesses the word first, wins the card. The player with the most cards at the end of the game wins. (Teacher selects the first card.) This word is a noun. It has two syllables. You would hear this word being used by an astronomer to describe a rare sight in the sky. A synonym for the word is amazing . . . (Player 2 interjects.) Is the target word astonishing? Yes! That's it!"	

WE DO (Teacher guides, supports, and assesses) *Lesson Checkpoint #1*	"It's your turn to practice! In front of you, you will find a stack of cue cards. Work with your partner to do your best to identify each word. When we are done, we will each take time to create a list of those words we feel like we might need to practice a bit more this year. Go ahead, begin, and have fun!" * *Lesson Checkpoint #1:* Ask yourself, "How am I actively engaging all learners? Are the students demonstrating the ability to complete the task and meet the goal of the lesson with peer and teacher support?"	The part of speech is . . . The number of syllables is . . . You would see or hear this word being used by . . . A synonym/antonym for this word is . . . The definition of this word is . . .
YOU DO (Teacher supports through individual and small group differentiated instruction and assesses students) *Lesson Checkpoint #2*	"Great collaboration! I see lots of evidence of your mastery of new words. What I'd like for you to do now is construct a list of words that you mastered and those words that you feel we might need to practice just a bit more." Student completes the activity individually. Lists are then gathered for future instruction.	
SHARE *Lesson Checkpoint #2*	Teacher structures a brief share of the learning activity.	

LIMITED ENGLISH PROFICIENCY:
LEVELED QUESTION SUPPORTS

Point to the word that matches this clue.

Find the word that means _____.

Match this clue card to the correct word.

Place the correct word next to this clue card.

Does this word match the clue _____?

Clue Cards

Target Word: _____	Target Word: _____	Target Word: _____
This word is a(n) _____. (Part of Speech)	This word is a(n) _____. (Part of Speech)	This word is a(n) _____. (Part of Speech)
This word has __syllables.	This word has __syllables.	This word has __syllables.
You would see or hear this word being used by _____.	You would see or hear this word being used by _____.	You would see or hear this word being used by _____.
A synonym/antonym for this word is _____.	A synonym/antonym for this word is _____.	A synonym/antonym for this word is _____.
The definition of this word is _____ _____ _____ _____.	The definition of this word is _____ _____ _____ _____.	The definition of this word is _____ _____ _____ _____.
Target Word: _____	Target Word: _____	Target Word: _____
This word is a(n) _____. (Part of Speech)	This word is a(n) _____. (Part of Speech)	This word is a(n) _____. (Part of Speech)
This word has __syllables.	This word has __syllables.	This word has __syllables.
You would see or hear this word being used by _____.	You would see or hear this word being used by _____.	You would see or hear this word being used by _____.
A synonym/antonym for this word is _____.	A synonym/antonym for this word is _____.	A synonym/antonym for this word is _____.
The definition of this word is _____ _____ _____ _____.	The definition of this word is _____ _____ _____ _____.	The definition of this word is _____ _____ _____ _____.

Target Word: _____	Target Word: _____	Target Word: _____
This word is a(n) _____. (Part of Speech)	This word is a(n) _____. (Part of Speech)	This word is a(n)_____. (Part of Speech)
This word has __syllables.	This word has __syllables.	This word has __syllables.
You would see or hear this word being used by _____.	You would see or hear this word being used by _____.	You would see or hear this word being used by _____.
A synonym/antonym for this word is _____.	A synonym/antonym for this word is _____.	A synonym/antonym for this word is _____.
The definition of this word is _____ _____ _____ _____.	The definition of this word is _____ _____ _____ _____.	The definition of this word is _____ _____ _____ _____.

Mini-lesson Title: He Said, She Said

Questions to keep in mind:
* Assessment: How will I know if the students have achieved the goal of the lesson? What will I observe or collect?
* Lesson Checkpoint #1 (During the Lesson): Am I actively engaging all learners? What evidence will I look for (observation) to assess if the students are meeting the goal of the lesson?
* Lesson Checkpoint #2 (At the end of independent work time/Exit Slip): What evidence will I collect to assess if the students are meeting the goal of the lesson?

Lesson Segment	Teaching Moves (Instruction may sound like . . .)	Language Production Sentence Frames
Introduce and Connect	"We've been working on understanding and remembering a few new words this week. Many of you have shared what you think it means to know a word. You have said that knowing a word means being able to define it or to tell someone what it means."	
	"That is just one part of it! Knowing a word well means you can explain what it means, use it in a sentence, and be able to recognize it when people use it in different ways."	
	"Today I'm going to show you how to use what we know about the meaning of a word to create sentences about the way each word could be used. People use words in different ways. Word use depends on who is using it, and when and where it's being used."	
I DO (Teacher models)	"I'm going to show you how I would use the 'He Said/She Said' graphic organizer to help me use our words a few different ways. Because one part of our activity requires me to work with a partner, I'm going to demonstrate the lesson with my partner, Bobby."	When I use the He Said, She Said strategy, I . . .
	"We are going to start with the word *artifact*. The teacher said, 'There are many artifacts on display at the museum.' Let me write that down in the second column. Now it says, 'partner sentence.' How would you use this word in a sentence?" (*Teacher writes partner sentence.*)	In the first column, I . . . In the second column, I . . . In the last column, I . . .

WE DO (Teacher guides, supports, and assesses) *Lesson Checkpoint #1*	"It's your turn to practice. Work with your partner to work with our other new word, *unearth*. Be sure to follow the graphic organizer and complete each column. Enjoy your conversations with one another about all of our new words!" *(Teacher circulates, assesses. Teacher also can modify use of the strategy by chunking the tasks. This would require that students complete each segment of the graphic organizer step by step, with teachers calling the group back together after each step.)* * *Lesson Checkpoint #1:* Ask yourself, "Are the students demonstrating the ability to complete the task and meet the goal of the lesson with peer and teacher support?"	My partner's sentence is . . . My sentence is . . . I think _____ would use this word because . . .
YOU DO (Teacher supports through individual and small group differentiated instruction and assesses students) *Lesson Checkpoint #2*	"Fantastic! Each of you is going to try it on your own now. Remember, we are going to gather together again in a few minutes to share our work with each other." Student completes the activity individually. Students who displayed evidence of needing additional assistance can be provided with a brief targeted reteach of the activity or key concepts within the activity based on the data gathered during *Lesson Checkpoint 1.	
SHARE *Lesson Checkpoint #2*	Teacher structures an opportunity for students to celebrate their work.	

(Chung 2012)

LIMITED ENGLISH PROFICIENCY:
LEVELED QUESTION SUPPORTS

Point to your partner's sentence. Read your partners sentence.
Place the word next to the sketch of a person who might use this word.
Is this a word that a _____ or _____ would use?

He Said/She Said

*Ask myself, "How would different people use this word?"

Word	My teacher said . . .	My partner said . . .	_____ said . . .

Mini-lesson Title: He Said, She Said

Questions to keep in mind:

* Assessment: How will I know if the students have achieved the goal of the lesson? What will I observe or collect?
* Lesson Checkpoint #1 (During the Lesson): Am I actively engaging all learners? What evidence will I look for (observation) to assess if the students are meeting the goal of the lesson?
* Lesson Checkpoint #2 (At the end of independent work time/Exit Slip): What evidence will I collect to assess if the students are meeting the goal of the lesson?

Lesson Segment	Teaching Moves (Instruction may sound like . . .)	Language Production Sentence Frames
Introduce and Connect	"Today we are going to create a tool called a Jumper that we can use to improve our word choices and the quality words that we use when we are writing. We can accomplish this by using one of our favorite reference tools, a Thesaurus. We know that a thesaurus can be used to help us find synonyms and antonyms for common or overused words." "If we look up overused words to find alternatives, we may be able to grow our vocabularies by substituting old words with more interesting and sophisticated words. We can add these words to our writing and use them in conversations, too."	A thesaurus is a reference tool that . . . A synonym is . . . .
I DO (Teacher models)	"I'm going to show you exactly how I would create a Jumper before I ask you to try it with your partner. I begin by writing a commonly overused word in the star at the top. For this lesson, I will demonstrate using the word *said*. I use the word *said* all of the time when I refer to a person's oral response or spoken words." "Watch me use my thesaurus to find synonyms or words that I could use to replace the word *said* the next time I overuse it." "Notice how I use what I know about the order of letters in the alphabet and the guide words located at the top corner of each page to help me find the overused word and a list of synonyms that are related."	When I use the jumper strategy, I . . . I use the thesaurus to . . . .

(continued)

Lesson Segment	Teaching Moves (Instruction may sound like . . .)	Language Production Sentence Frames
I DO (Teacher models)	"Let's see, I open up my thesaurus and look for words that start with 'S' because *said* begins with that letter. 'S' comes after 'R' and before 'T,' so that should help me. Here! I found 'S' words! (*Teacher skims the thesaurus until the word it is located.*) Aha! Found it!" "Synonyms I could use to substitute the overuse of the word *said* are: *recite, repeat, utter, deliver, perform, declaim,* and *orate*. Let me write those words on each line of the Jumper." (*Teacher demonstrates adding the synonyms to the Jumper.*) "Did you all see how I used my thesaurus to help me find a few synonyms I can start using to help me avoid using the same word all of the time?"	When I use the jumper strategy, I . . . I use the thesaurus to . . .
WE DO (Teacher guides, supports, and assesses) *Lesson Checkpoint #1	"Now, before you create one on your own, lets create one together. I have noticed that many of you overuse the word *exciting* in either your writing or your conversations." "Use a thesaurus with your partner to locate synonyms you could add to your practice Jumper. I'm going to come around to help and coach each of you to successfully complete this activity." * *Lesson Checkpoint #1:* Ask yourself, "Am I actively engaging all learners? Are the students demonstrating the ability to complete the task and meet the goal of the lesson with peer and teacher support?"	The overused word is . . . One synonym is . . . Another synonym is . . . .
YOU DO (Teacher supports through individual and small group differentiated instruction and assesses students) *Lesson Checkpoint #2	"You all did such a fantastic job! Now you will try a few more on your own." Student completes the activity individually. Students who displayed evidence of needing additional assistance can be provided with a brief targeted reteach of the activity or key concepts within the activity based on the data gathered during *Lesson Checkpoint 1.	
SHARE *Lesson Checkpoint #2	Teacher structures an opportunity to share and celebrate student work.	

LIMITED ENGLISH PROFICIENCY:
LEVELED QUESTION SUPPORTS

Point to the thesaurus. Point to the synonym. Point to another synonym.
Find the overused word. Find a synonym. Find another synonym.
Match the overused word to the synonym.
Place the synonym next to the overused word.
Is _____ or _____ a synonym for the overused word?

Jumper Lesson Template

*Place the target word in the star burst and the synonyms for the word on each of the lines. The opposite side can be used to collect antonyms!

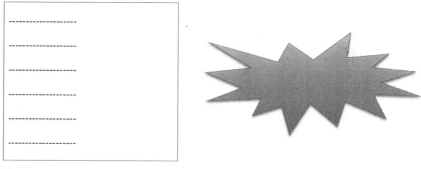

Figure 3.1.

Mini-lesson Title: Recycling Word Parts

Questions to keep in mind:
* Assessment: How will I know if the students have achieved the goal of the lesson? What will I observe or collect?
* Lesson Checkpoint #1 (During the Lesson): Am I actively engaging all learners? What evidence will I look for (observation) to assess if the students are meeting the goal of the lesson?
* Lesson Checkpoint #2 (At the end of independent work time/Exit Slip): What evidence will I collect to assess if the students are meeting the goal of the lesson?

Lesson Segment	Teaching Moves (Instruction may sound like . . .)	Language Production Sentence Frames
Introduce and Connect	"We have been learning that even the small parts of words can be very meaningful. We know to look for prefixes, suffixes, roots, and words within words to help us figure out the meaning of a word we don't know." "Today we are going to practice finding prefixes, suffixes, roots, and words within words as part of a word play activity called Recycling Word Parts. Once we identify a meaningful part of a word, we can use that part to create a list of words that we know that contain that part too!"	A prefix is . . . A suffix is . . . . A root is . . . .
I DO (Teacher models)	"Before you try it out, I want you to watch me model it. Here's my Recycling Word Parts graphic organizer." (The teacher takes on the role of a student and displays the chart for the class/group and thinks aloud.) "I noticed that the teacher placed the target word in the boxes at the top. Today the word in the box that I'm going to recycle is discovered. I see the prefix dis– in the word. Well, I know that when the prefix dis– is added to a word it means not or the opposite of the word." "I also see the word cover hidden within this word. (Teacher points out each part.) I know a bunch of other words that have the word cover in them. Last, I notice the suffix –ed. I know that when I add the –ed suffix to a word it becomes a past tense verb."	When I use the Recycling Word Parts graphic organizer, I . . . First, I . . . . Then, I . . . . Finally, I . . . .

I DO (Teacher models)	"Now that I've identified the meaningful parts, I'm going to recycle them to create some new words. So, in the first column I'm going list words that begin with the prefix *dis*–. Hmm, I know! One new word with the prefix *dis*– is *disconnect*. I'm going to write that down on my graphic organizer." "Next, I'm going to write the word I found within the target word in the second column. That word is *cover*. Another word that I know with the word *cover* is *uncovering*! I'm going to add that to my organizer too." "Last, I'm going to begin the list of words with the suffix –*ed* in them. I know! Instead of the word *uncovering*, I can drop the –*ing* to add –*ed* creating the word *uncovered*." *(Teacher adds the word to the last column of the organizer.)* "Did you see how I used the meaningful parts of the target words to create new words?"	
WE DO (Teacher guides, supports, and assesses) *Lesson Checkpoint #1*	"Before you go off to work on this activity alone, I want you to try it with the help of your partner and with me right here coaching you. You can work off of the list I started for you using the prefix *dis*–, the word *cover*, and the suffix –*ed*." *(The teacher meets with partnerships to support students and finds the work of a partnership to highlight and share with the class.)* "Theresa and Robert have a few great words they would like to share with everyone and add to my Recycling Word Parts graphic organizer. For the prefix *dis*– they came up with the word *disappear*. Let me add that to my organizer."	The prefix we added is . . . The suffix we added is . . . Our new recycled word is . . .

(continued)

Lesson Segment	Teaching Moves (Instruction may sound like . . .)	Language Production Sentence Frames
WE DO (Teacher guides, supports, and assesses) *Lesson Checkpoint #1	"Using the word cover they were able to add on to create the word *recovering*. And finally, they chose to drop the *–ing* from recovering and add *–ed* to make the word *recovered*. I'm going to add those awesome words too! Great job!" "Let's see how many more words you can create now by recycling. You can work independently or with a partner for the next 10 minutes to create a full list of words. Then we will gather together again to share all of our lists!" * *Lesson Checkpoint #1:* Ask yourself, "Am I actively engaging all learners? Are the students demonstrating the ability to complete the task and meet the goal of the lesson with peer and teacher support?"	The prefix we added is . . . The suffix we added is . . . Our new recycled word is . . .
YOU DO (Teacher supports through individual and small group differentiated instruction and assesses students) *Lesson Checkpoint #2	"Such excellent work! Now you will try a few more on your own. We will gather again in a little while to share our graphic organizers with our partners, small groups, etc." Student completes the activity individually. Students who displayed evidence of needing additional assistance can be provided with a brief targeted reteach of the activity or key concepts within the activity based on the data gathered during *Lesson Checkpoint 1.	
SHARE *Lesson Checkpoint #2	Teacher structures a brief group share of student work.	

LIMITED ENGLISH PROFICIENCY:
LEVELED QUESTION SUPPORTS

Point to the prefix. Point to the suffix. Point to the root.
Find the prefix. Point to the suffix. Point to the root.
Match the prefix to the root. Match the suffix to the root.
Place the prefix next to the root. Place the suffix next to the root.
Is this a prefix? Is this a suffix? Is this a root?
Is _____, a prefix, suffix, or root?

Recycling Word Parts

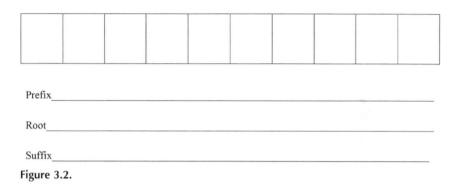

Prefix_____

Root_____

Suffix_____

Figure 3.2.

Mini-lesson Title: Relay Stories

Questions to keep in mind:
* Assessment: How will I know if the students have achieved the goal of the lesson? What will I observe or collect?
* Lesson Checkpoint #1 (During the Lesson): Am I actively engaging all learners? What evidence will I look for (observation) to assess if the students are meeting the goal of the lesson?
* Lesson Checkpoint #2 (At the end of independent work time/Exit Slip): What evidence will I collect to assess if the students are meeting the goal of the lesson?

Lesson Segment	Teaching Moves (Instruction may sound like . . .)	Language Production Sentence Frames
Introduce and Connect	"We have been working on learning words in so many ways. We know we should be revisiting and using words frequently because the more we use it, the better chance we have of adding it to our permanent vocabulary. Today I want to show you another fun way we could work together to revisit and review words we've already learned by creating Relay Stories." "Creating Relay Stories are a bit like running in a relay race. Our goal is to work as a team to use a group of words—some we have learned recently, and others we have learned throughout this school year—to create a story." "We take turns passing our pencil from one team member to another, each of us adding on a sentence using a target vocabulary word to build a story. We will know we have reached the finish line when we have used all of the target words."	A relay is . . .
I DO (Teacher models)	"Before you have a chance to try it with your groups, let's try one together. I'm going to ask for a few volunteers to help me demonstrate how to complete this activity. I'm going to pretend to be a student in this class working with a group of my friends to complete a vocabulary story. Who wants to try it out with me?" "Great! Come up and join me Theresa, Deanna, and Miles." *(Teacher whispers to talk with the group about the activity before demonstrating for the class.)*	When we complete the relay story, we . . . First, ... Then, ... Finally, ...

"Watch us try it using the words listed in the word bank of the organizer. Listen closely as the first group member begins the story using the sentence starter the teacher placed in the box at the top."

"Pay attention to the way we construct a story by passing the pencil around the circle, each of us adding a sentence that includes a word listed at the top of the graphic organizer." *(Teacher and students use the fishbowl method to demonstrate the shared construction of a story using target vocabulary words.)*

"You will notice that constructing a Relay Story is somewhat similar to playing in a relay race. In a relay race, participants work as part of a team running and passing a baton to share the responsibility of crossing a finish line. Similarly, when constructing a Relay Story, participants work as part of a group or team to share the responsibility of passing a pencil to meet the goal of using target words in sentences creating a story."

"Let's get started. Can I go first? *(Teacher asks group members.)* Great! Our teacher has posted the target words we should try to use for our story."

"The first few are *appalled, divert, comet,* and *prominent.* Theresa, can you pass me the pencil so I can begin our Relay Story? I'm going to start with the target word *comet.* My sentence is, 'I would give anything in the world to see a *comet* flying across the night sky.' Here Theresa, you try next!" *(Teacher passes the pencil to the next group member.)*

"I have heard that to see a *comet* fly across the sky, people should observe the sky at 11 p.m. when it would be most *prominent.* Let me add that sentence onto the graphic organizer." *(Theresa adds on her sentence and passes the pencil to Miles.)*

"I'm going to add on a sentence using the word *appalled.* 'I would be *appalled* if I sat out all night hoping to see the *comet* and an unexpected event prevented me from viewing it!'" *(Miles adds on his sentence and passes the pencil to Deanna.)*

(continued)

Lesson Segment	Teaching Moves (Instruction may sound like . . .)	Language Production Sentence Frames
I DO (Teacher models)	"Because the word *divert* is the only word left, I will add on a sentence using that word. Give me a second to think about what objects in space may make a *comet divert* from its course." *(Deanna takes an extended pause to think.)* "I've got it! I'm going to add on the sentence, 'The most likely event that could prevent me from viewing a *comet* would be if another space object was directly in its path and caused the comet to *divert* off its original path.' Let me add that onto the other sentences." *(Deanna adds her sentence onto the Relay Story graphic organizer.)* *(The teacher ends the fishbowl instruction to speak directly to the listeners.)* "Did you see how we took turns to share the responsibility of creating a story using our target vocabulary?"	When we complete the relay story, we . . . First, . . . Then, . . . Finally, . . .
WE DO (Teacher guides, supports, and assesses) *Lesson Checkpoint #1	"Let's try to write a short Relay Story right now using a few more words we've learned this year. Create a small group with the classmates you are sitting near, maybe four or five of you; then we can get started." *(Teacher waits a minute for the students to form groups.)* "Great! Now it's time to begin. I would like you to work with your group to create a short Relay Story using the five words I have posted up here." *(Teacher points to the words posted for all students to see)*	

	"I will hand one copy of the Relay Story graphic organizer out to each group. You are free to choose any story starter you like. To make it a bit more fun this time, I'm going to set the timer for three minutes. Let's see who finishes first!" "When all of you have finished, you will have a chance to share your stories. Get ready. Get set. Begin! (*The teacher moves from group to group listening in and coaches students as needed.*) * *Lesson Checkpoint #1*: Ask yourself, "Am I actively engaging all learners? Are the students demonstrating the ability to complete the task and meet the goal of the lesson with peer and teacher support?"	
YOU DO (Teacher supports through individual and small group differentiated instruction and assesses students) **Lesson Checkpoint #2*	"Your stories were fantastic! The best part of listening to all of you work together was the laughter in each group. I'm so glad this activity is fun for you to complete!" "Because you did such a great job trying it out, I'm thinking you will love trying it again using a longer list of words. I have posted ten new target vocabulary words I would like each group to include in their stories. (*Teacher points to the posted words.*) I will give you some more time, allowing you the opportunity to create a great story that you will be proud to share with the class." "We will gather together to share before the end of class. Have fun!"	
SHARE **Lesson Checkpoint #2*	Teacher structures an opportunity for groups to briefly share their relay stories.	

(August and Snow 2007; Chung 2012; Vaughn-Shavuo 1990)

LIMITED ENGLISH PROFICIENCY:
LEVELED QUESTION SUPPORTS

Point to the word _____.
Find the word _____.
Should we use the word _____ or _____ in this sentence?
Would you use the word _____ or _____ in this sentence?

Relay Story

Choose a story starter below.	Target Words
• I never thought it would be possible, but there I was… • I'd give anything in the world to see… • I walked into the room and…	

Title-_____

Authors_____

_____

_____

_____

_____

_____

_____

_____

_____

_____

_____

_____

_____

Figure 3.3.

Mini-lesson Title: Welcome to My World, Word!

Questions to keep in mind:

* Assessment: How will I know if the students have achieved the goal of the lesson? What will I observe or collect?
* Lesson Checkpoint #1 (During the Lesson): Am I actively engaging all learners? What evidence will I look for (observation) to assess if the students are meeting the goal of the lesson?
* Lesson Checkpoint #2 (At the end of independent work time/Exit Slip): What evidence will I collect to assess if the students are meeting the goal of the lesson?

Lesson Segment	Teaching Moves (Instruction may sound like . . .)	Language Production Sentence Frames
Introduce and Connect	"We know that really knowing a word doesn't just mean we can define it; it means that we can use it automatically in our conversations with others and in our writing."	
I DO (Teacher models)	"As always, I'm going to show you how I push myself to get to know a word better by thinking more about it. Using the Welcome to my World, Word! Graphic organizer as a guide, I'm going to define, relate, apply, personally connect and create using one of our new vocabulary words."	When I use the Welcome to My World, Word! strategy, I . . .
	"Here is my graphic organizer. (Teacher displays a copy.) Notice how I write my target word in the middle circle. Then, I follow the boxes clockwise to help me think about the word in different ways. Listen closely because I'm going to share my thinking with you as I fill in each box."	
	"Ok, the word I was introduced to yesterday was comet. The first box says, 'I can define the word.' I can because I learned about it yesterday. I'm going to write that a comet is an object we can see in the sky. It is made up of ice and dust particles, and it looks like it has a tail when it gets close to the sun."	
	"On to box 2. It says, 'I can associate this word with other words.' Hmmm, this word makes me think of the words outer space, planets, stars, and orbiting. Let me write that down in the box." (Teacher demonstrates filling in the graphic organizer.)	

(continued)

Lesson Segment	Teaching Moves (Instruction may sound like . . .)	Language Production Sentence Frames
I DO (Teacher models)	"Moving along to box 3. Box 3 says I can apply this word. When would I use this word? I know! I would use this word in science class or if I were teaching a friend about objects found in space." "The next box (4) says, 'I can connect this word to myself if I think of . . .' That's helpful. I can connect to this word personally. *Cometa* in English can be translated to *cometa* in Spanish. The words sound very alike. That should make it easier to understand. Let me write that down." "Last, I reach box 5. Box 5 says, 'I can create what I envision when I think of this word by sketching it.' Hmm, let me think about this for a second. *(Teacher closes eyes to envision.)* I can see a *comet* in my mind. It looks like a giant ice ball flying through space. I'm going to make a quick sketch to get it out of my head and onto paper." "Wow! I'm done! I have certainly worked to get to know this word better by following the graphic organizer! So fun!"	When I use the Welcome to My World, Word! strategy, I . . .
WE DO (Teacher guides, supports, and assesses) *Lesson Checkpoint #1	"It's your turn to practice! I would like for you and your partner to welcome the words to your world. I would like for you to practice with another word we discussed this week, *astonishing*."	The target word is . . . My definition of ___ is . . . I can associate the word ___ with ___.

	(Teacher circulates, assesses. Teacher also can modify use of the strategy by chunking the tasks. This would require that students complete each segment of the graphic organizer step by step, with teachers calling the group back together after each step.) * Lesson Checkpoint #1: Ask yourself, "How am I actively engaging all learners? Are the students demonstrating the ability to complete the task and meet the goal of the lesson with peer and teacher support?"	I might use this word when . . . I can personally connect to this word because . . . My sketch of the word ___ includes . . .
YOU DO (Teacher supports through individual and small group differentiated instruction and assesses students) *Lesson Checkpoint #2	"Bravo, everyone! Now you will try one on your own. We will gather again in a little while to share our graphic organizers with our partners, small groups, etc." Student completes the activity individually. Students who displayed evidence of needing additional assistance can be provided with a brief targeted reteach of the activity or key concepts within the activity based on the data gathered during *Lesson Checkpoint 1.	
SHARE *Lesson Checkpoint #2	Teacher structures a group share.	

LIMITED ENGLISH PROFICIENCY:
LEVELED QUESTION SUPPORTS

Point to the word that can be linked to the target word.
Would you say that _____ and _____ are the same?
Match the target word to a word that is the same.
Place the target word next to a word that is the same.
Can you use this word to describe your ____ or _____?

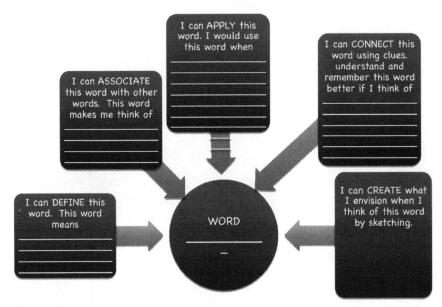

Figure 3.4.

Mini-lesson Title: Word Building

Questions to keep in mind:

* Assessment: How will I know if the students have achieved the goal of the lesson? What will I observe or collect?
* Lesson Checkpoint #1 (During the Lesson): Am I actively engaging all learners? What evidence will I look for (observation) to assess if the students are meeting the goal of the lesson?
* Lesson Checkpoint #2 (At the end of independent work time/Exit Slip): What evidence will I collect to assess if the students are meeting the goal of the lesson?

Lesson Segment	Teaching Moves (Instruction may sound like . . .)	Language Production Sentence Frames
Introduce and Connect	"We have been learning how prefixes and suffixes can help us figure out the meaning of an unknown word. Today I'm going to show you how we can use the Word Builder graphic organizer to help us grow one word into many by adding on the prefixes and suffixes we have been learning."	
I DO (Teacher models)	"Let me show you how I would use the word-building graphic organizer to create a list of words from one target word. For my demonstration, I'm going to try it using the word *cover* as my target word. Pay close attention to the way I use the graphic organizer as a guide to help me grow my word."	When I use the Word Builder, I . . . First, I . . . Then, I . . . Lastly, I . . .
	"I see that the heading at the top of the first column says, 'What could be added on to change the word?' Hmmm, let me think about this for a second." *(Teacher thinks aloud.)* "Which prefix have I learned that could be added on here? I know! I can add the prefix *dis–*. Let me write *dis–* in the first column."	
	"If I move over to the second column, I notice that it asks me what the word becomes. The word *cover* becomes the word *discover* after I add the prefix *dis*."	
	"Moving onto the last column, it asks, 'How can you use the word in a sentence?' Hmmm, I'm going to create a great one! Watch me add my sentence to the graphic organizer." *(The teacher shares the sentence aloud while writing it on the graphic organizer.)* "The explorer sought to discover a new land."	
	"I did it!"	

(continued)

Lesson Segment	Teaching Moves (Instruction may sound like . . .)	Language Production Sentence Frames
WE DO (Teacher guides, supports, and assesses) *Lesson Checkpoint #1	"We should keep on going. This time, it's your turn. Talk with your partner to figure out another prefix or suffix you could add on to our target word (cover) to create a new word. Once you have the prefix or suffix, hold up your wipe board so that I can see!" (Teacher monitors student responses.) "Great! Now, think of a sentence you could use the word in. I'm going to come around to listen and coach any group that needs me." (After a minute or two, the teacher highlights the work of a few students and adds their ideas to the Word Builder graphic organizer used in the demonstration.) * Lesson Checkpoint #1: Ask yourself, "Am I actively engaging all learners? Are the students demonstrating the ability to complete the task and meet the goal of the lesson with peer and teacher support?"	Our target word is . . . We added the prefix/ suffix . . . Our new word is . . . One example of a sentence using this word is . . .
YOU DO (Teacher supports through individual and small group differentiated instruction and assesses students) *Lesson Checkpoint #2	"You have all done a great job! I think you are ready to go and try to do this activity on your own. Here are a few more examples to try." Student completes the activity individually. Students who displayed evidence of needing additional assistance can be provided with a brief targeted reteach of the activity or key concepts within the activity based on the data gathered during *Lesson Checkpoint 1.	
SHARE *Lesson Checkpoint #2	Teacher structures a group or pair share.	

LIMITED ENGLISH PROFICIENCY:
LEVELED QUESTION SUPPORTS

Point to the prefix. Point to the suffix. Point to the root.
Find the prefix. Point to the suffix. Point to the root.
Match the prefix to the root. Match the suffix to the root.
Place the prefix next to the root. Place the suffix next to the root.
Is this a prefix? Is this a suffix? Is this a root?
Is _____, a prefix, suffix, or root?
Is the new word _____ or _____?
Would _____ be a good example of a sentence using the new word?

Word Building

Target Word
_____

What prefix or suffix could be added on to change the word?	What does the word become?	How can you use the word in a sentence?

More with Morphemes!

What:
If–Then Morphology Magic

Why:
The use of morphology offers students another avenue for learning the depth and breadth of vocabulary development. This is an exercise in determining how prefixes and suffixes change the meaning of the root word.

How:

1. Students receive direct explicit instruction about the purpose and function of prefixes and suffixes.
2. The teacher models an if–then example and explains how the prefix or suffix changes the meaning of the root word and in the case of a suffix, its part of speech.
3. The students are grouped and given a task card.

> If the prefix *post* means after, then *postdate* means . . .
> then *postgame* means . . .
> then *postmeridian* means . . .
> then *postscript* means . . .
>
> If *hood* means state or quality of being, then *childhood* means . . .
> then *falsehood* means . . .
> then *statehood* means . . .
> then *sainthood* means . . .

4. Then each person in the group takes a word can completes the if–then phrase.
5. Each student explains to his or her group how the prefix or suffix changes the meaning of the root word and its part of speech.
6. Finally, the students use the word correctly in a discussion about the word.
7. For an added challenge, students locate four additional words that can fit the same if–then phrase with the given prefix or suffix and use them correctly in a written sentence.

What:
Matching Morphemes and Models

Why:

Picture clues can often bridge the gap between words and understanding concepts. Here students use illustrations to depict the meaning of affixes. For students who are developing the concept of morphemes, pictures can lead the way.

How:

1. The teacher selects a series of suffixes and picture models that illustrate the meaning of the suffix.
2. Through a discussion about the pictures used as models, the students can determine the meaning of the suffix.

   T: Can anyone explain what we see in this picture?

   S: A cheetah.

   T: Can you tell me more about what the cheetah is doing?

   S: The cheetah is running very fast.

   T: That is correct. Did you know that the cheetah is the fastest animal on land?

   T: Can anyone find the word that describes the cheetah?

   S: Yes, the word fastest.

   T: Let's look at the word. What part of the word tells us it is the fastest?

   S: –est

   T: So, what do you think the meaning of the suffix –est means?

   S: It's the most fast?

   T: That's correct! We use –est to mean the most.

3. The students are to find three additional pictures that would portray the same meaning of a word with the suffix *–est*, share their pictures, and orally use the words correctly in a sentence.

What:
Which would you rather be?

Why:
Many times students have to describe characters in a story or compare characters in the story but are unfamiliar with words used to describe these traits.

Within this activity, students are provided with a choice of character traits and asked to decide which they would rather be.

How:

1. Teacher selects a series of paired words and asks the students to decide, based on the prefix/suffix they see, which one they would rather be.

   T: Which would you rather be and why?

   a. perplexed or enlightened

   b. serene or belligerent

   c. gallant or apprehensive

   d. magnanimous or stingy

   e. intelligent or cunning

   f. aloof or involved

2. Students are then asked to locate the prefix or suffix within each word and use these word parts to assist in defining the meaning of each trait. After learning more about the meaning of the trait, students must justify why they did or did not choose specific options.
3. As an extension, students might link each characteristic to texts read within class or in other content area classrooms. Students might also describe familiar people using these traits, as well.

References

August, D., M. Carlo, C. Dressler, and C. Snow. 2005. "The Critical Role of Vocabulary Development for English Language Learners." *Learning Disabilities Research & Practice* 20 (1): 50–57.

August, D., P. McCardle, and T. Shanahan. 2014. "Developing Literacy in English Language Learners: Findings from a Review of the Experimental Research." *School Psychology Review* 43 (4): 490–498.

Beck, I., M. G. McKeown, and L. Kucan. 2002. *Bringing Words to Life: Robust Vocabulary Development*. New York: Guilford.

Beck, I. L., M. G. McKeown, and L. Kucan. 2013. *Bringing Words to Life: Robust Vocabulary Instruction*, 2nd ed. New York: Guilford Press.

Biemiller, A., and C. Boote. 2006. "An Effective Method for Building Meaning Vocabulary in Primary Grades." *Journal of Educational Psychology* 98 (1): 44.

Blachowicz, C. L., P. J. Fisher, D. Ogle, and S. Watts-Taffe. 2006. "Vocabulary: Questions from the Classroom." *Reading Research Quarterly* 41 (4): 524–539.

Carlo, M. S., D. August, B. McLaughlin, C. E. Snow, C. Dressler, D. N. Lippman, T. J. Lively, and C. E. White. 2004. "Closing the Gap: Addressing the Vocabulary Needs of English-language Learners in Bilingual and Mainstream Classrooms." *Reading Research Quarterly* 39 (2): 188–215.

Chung, S. F. 2012. "Research-based Vocabulary Instruction for English Language Learners." *Reading* 12 (2): 105–120.

Cummins, J. 2008. "BICS and CALP: Empirical and Theoretical Status of the Distinction." In *Encyclopedia of Language and Education*, edited by Nancy Hornberg, 487–499. New York: Springer.

Gersten, R., and S. Baker. 2000. "What We Know about Effective Instructional Practices for English-language Learners." *Exceptional Children* 66 (4): 454–470.

Goldenberg, C. 2008. "Teaching English Language Learners What the Research Does—and Does Not—Say." *American Education*, 8–44.

Graves, M. F. 2009. "Essential Readings on Vocabulary Instruction." *Reading Today* 26 (6): 26.

Hart, B., and T. R. Risley. 2003. "The Early Catastrophe: The 30 Million Word Gap by Age 3." *American Educator* 27 (1): 4–9.

Krashen, S. D. 1987. *Principles and Practices in Second Language Acquisition.* New York: Prentice-Hall.

Manyak, P. C., and E. B. Bauer. 2009. "English Vocabulary Instruction for English Learners." *The Reading Teacher* 63 (2): 174–176.

McKeown, M. G., I. L. Beck, R. C. Omanson, and M. T. Pople. 1985. "Some Effects of the Nature and Frequency of Vocabulary Instruction on the Knowledge and Use of Words." *Reading Research Quarterly,* 522–535.

Nagy, W. E., and J. A. Scott. 2000. "Vocabulary Processes." *Handbook of Reading Research* 3: 269–284.

Pearson, P. D., and M. C. Gallagher. 1983. "The Instruction of Reading Comprehension." *Contemporary Educational Psychology* 8 (3): 317–344.

Rosenshine, B. 1983. "Teaching Functions in Instructional Programs." *The Elementary School Journal* 83 (4): 335–351.

Shanahan, T., and D. August. 2006. *Report of the National Literacy Panel: Research on Teaching Reading to English Language Learners.* Mahwah, NJ: Erlbaum.

Silverman, R., and S. Hines. 2009. "The Effects of Multimedia-enhanced Instruction on the Vocabulary of English-language Learners and Non-English-language Learners in Pre-kindergarten through Second Grade." *Journal of Educational Psychology* 101 (2): 305.

Stanley, P. D., and D. W. Ginther. 1991. "The Effects of Purpose and Frequency on Vocabulary Learning from Written Context of High and Low Ability Reading Comprehenders." *Literacy Research and Instruction* 30 (4): 31–41.

Stanovich, K. 1986. "Matthew Effects in Reading: Some Consequences of Individual Differences in the Acquisition of Literacy." *Reading Research Quarterly* 21 (4): 360–407.

Taba, H. 1967. *Teacher's Handbook for Elementary Social Studies.* Reading, MA: Addison-Wesley.

Vaughn-Shavuo, F. 1990. *Using Story Grammar and Language Experience for Improving Recall and Comprehension in the Teaching of ESL to Spanish-dominant First-graders.* Available from ProQuest Dissertations & Theses Global. (303830655).

Zimmerman, B. J., and D. H. Schunk, eds. 2001. *Self-regulated Learning and Academic Achievement: Theoretical Perspectives.* New York: Routledge.

About the Authors

Melissa A. Parenti, EdD, earned her doctorate in teacher education in multicultural societies from the University of Southern California and is currently assistant teaching professor at Northeastern University. Her areas of expertise include preservice and in-service teacher preparation, instructional methodology, literacy, and support of English-language learners. Before beginning her role at the university level in 2011, Dr. Parenti served for fifteen years as a classroom teacher, reading specialist, and consultant in PK–12 school systems in Chicago, Los Angeles, and New York City. Her research is centered on improving the quality of instruction in high-need, low-resource schools in urban communities.

Danielle DiMarco, MS, is currently a doctoral candidate at St. John's University in New York. For nearly twenty years, she has worked in various capacities as a classroom teacher, staff developer, coach, and literacy consultant. Her teaching and consulting experience has allowed her to attain and share a wealth of knowledge in the field and has reached a widely receptive audience in New York City public and private schools, as well as districts servicing Long Island and Westchester County. Her research interests include best practices in literacy instruction, curriculum development, professional development, and professional-learning communities.

E. Francine Guastello, EdD, is associate professor of literacy, former chair of Human Services and Counseling, and coordinator of the Graduate Literacy Program at St. John's University in Queens, New York. Dr. Guastello is also a fellow in the Orton-Gillingham Academy of Practitioners and Educators and has been an educator for more than forty-five years. She was an elementary/junior high teacher, an elementary school principal, and, for the past eighteen years, she has been a part of the graduate literacy faculty at St. John's, specializing in the diagnosis and remediation of children and adults with learning disabilities. She instituted the first courses in multisensory language learning, providing intensive instruction for reading-specialist graduates enabling them to teach children and adults with dyslexia. She continues to serve as the co-project director of Project TIE: Training Innovative Educators, a grant-sponsored program conducting staff development in twenty-four low-achieving schools in Manhattan, Staten Island, Brooklyn, and Queens. She is also an educational evaluator and consultant to the School Sisters of Notre Dame's Educational Center for disenfranchised women preparing for the GED. Her research interests and professional publications include topics that focus on effective instructional practices in literacy development for low-achieving students, adults, and diverse learners and the promotion of family literacy. She is a co-author of *The Guided Reading: Kidstation Model.*